STEM
Waterworks

How Do DAMS Work?

Ryan Nagelhout

PowerKiDS press

New York

Published in 2017 by The Rosen Publishing Group, Inc.
29 East 21st Street, New York, NY 10010

First Edition

Editor: Greg Roza
Book Design: Mickey Harmon

Photo Credits: Cover, pp. 1–32 (water) elic/Shutterstock.com; cover, pp. 1–32 (pipes) Kovalenko Alexander/Shutterstock.com; cover (image) Alexander Lebedev/Shutterstock.com; p. 5 (inset) Adwo/Shutterstock.com; p. 5 (main) Lynn Y/Shutterstock.com; p. 7 Zelijko Radojko/Shutterstock.com; p. 9 https://upload.wikimedia.org/wikipedia/commons/thumb/f/f5/Embalse_romano_de_Proserpina.jpg/170px-Embalse_romano_de_Proserpina.jpg; p. 11 Ilko Iliev/Shutterstock.com; p. 13 (main) studio23/Shutterstock.com; p. 13 (lumber) pinyo bonmark/Shutterstock.com; p. 13 (steel) vvoe/Shutterstock.com; p. 13 (rocks) val lawless/Shutterstock.com; p. 15 Harald Sund/Photographer's Choice/Getty Images; p. 17 meanmachine77/Shutterstock.com; p. 21 Cloyd Teter/Contributor/Getty Images; p. 23 turtix/Shutterstock.com; p. 24 https://en.wikipedia.org/wiki/William_Mulholland#/media/File:William-Mulholland-in-1924.jpg; p. 25 https://upload.wikimedia.org/wikipedia/commons/3/3c/St._Francis_Dam_after_the_1928_failure.jpg; p. 27 corlaffra/Shutterstock.com; p. 29 Bloomberg/Contributor/Bloomberg/Getty Images.

Library of Congress Cataloging-in-Publication Data

Names: Nagelhout, Ryan, author.
Title: How do dams work? / Ryan Nagelhout.
Description: New York : PowerKids Press, [2016] | Series: STEM waterworks | Includes index.
Identifiers: LCCN 2016013444 | ISBN 9781499419993 (pbk.) | ISBN 9781499420012 (library bound) | ISBN 9781499420005 (6 pack)
Subjects: LCSH: Dams–Design and construction–Juvenile literature. | Dams–Environmental aspects–Juvenile literature. | Hydraulic engineering–Juvenile literature.
Classification: LCC TC540 .N24 2016 | DDC 627.8–dc23
LC record available at http://lccn.loc.gov/2016013444

Manufactured in the United States of America

CPSIA Compliance Information: Batch #BS16PK: For Further Information contact Rosen Publishing, New York, New York at 1-800-237-9932

Contents

Dam Animals 4

Why Dams? 6

Early History 8

How It Works 10

Dams Today 12

The Modern Build 14

Making Power 18

Reclamation 20

Hoover Dam 22

Mulholland Dive 24

The Lost Lake 26

When Dams Fail 28

Changing the Landscape 30

Glossary 31

Index 32

Websites 32

Dam Animals

Human inventions are often inspired by nature. For centuries people dreamed of crafting wings and taking flight. But the answer to human flight wasn't found in flapping. Science was needed to figure out how wings worked and how humans could engineer them and use them to fly.

Beaver dams, however, are an example of nature directly affecting the actions of humans. Stacking tree trunks and branches they've chewed down, beavers change the flow of water in their habitats. Humans soon learned the power their own dams could have—creating man-made lakes, altering rivers, and even generating electricity to provide power to homes and businesses. Human-built dams are some of the largest structures ever made. Let's explore the how and why of building dams and the impact these massive creations have on their surrounding **environment**.

In the Pipe

People learned about dams by watching beavers. Beavers use stones to weigh down the base of their dams, then interlock pieces of timber to make the walls. They use mud from the bottom of waterways to make their dams waterproof.

Dams are a good topic to study if you want to learn about STEM— science, technology, engineering, and math.

Why Dams?

Beavers and humans make dams for the same reason: to have a safe habitat to live in. Beaver dams create wetlands, which are a kind of habitat where many fish and other animals live. These wetlands also protect areas around rivers and streams during heavy rains by preventing floods and improving water quality.

Humans use dams to prevent downstream flooding as well. These massive dams hold back the flow of water, creating a large **reservoir** behind the dam. The reservoir's water can be used for recreation such as boating or fishing, but it can also be saved for communities to use for drinking, bathing, and watering plants. Dams can even be engineered to generate power. Dam water can be led to **hydroelectric** power plants, which use falling water to spin **turbines** and create electricity.

Man-made dams are easy to spot in nature because they usually create a reservoir of water behind their large walls.

A good dam can last a long time. Some dams built thousands of years ago are still in use today. The oldest working dam in the world is the Lake Homs Dam in Syria. It was built between 1319 and 1304 BC. The Proserpina Dam in Spain is the second oldest. Built in the first century AD, it is about 1,400 feet (427 m) long and 40 feet (12.2 m) tall.

The design of these early dams was simple: block the flow of a body of water with stone and soil and cover the dam in concrete. This kind of dam is called a gravity dam because it uses the size, weight, and strength of its rock and concrete to keep back the flow of water to form a reservoir.

Proserpina Dam is one of several gravity dams built by the Romans that are still used today.

Dams stop water from flowing, but for humans, building a dam is a bit more difficult than just piling up a bunch of dirt and tree branches. Dams need to be waterproof, strong, and designed so water can be let through in case of emergencies.

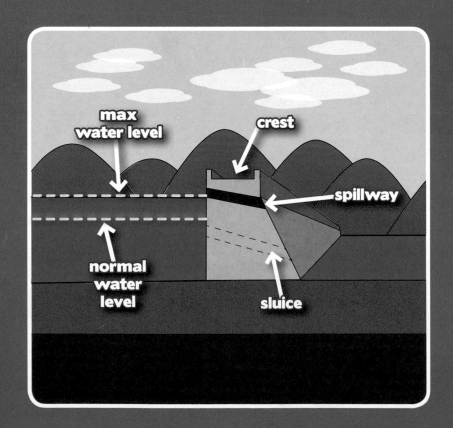

The part of the dam holding back water must be impermeable. That means it won't allow liquid to pass through it. Engineers must use materials that don't absorb water when building a dam.

The type of dam built often depends on the geography of the area around the dam. A sluice is a channel that passes through a dam with a gate at one end. It's used to control the flow of water. Sluice gates can be opened to let water pass through the channel in case levels get too high. Other channels, called spillways, let water flow over, around, or through the dam if water levels behind it rise too high.

Dams Today

Dams are often defined by their use. Storage dams are the most common type and are used to trap water for later use. They also store water for hydroelectric power and to protect against flooding. **Diversion** dams block the normal path of a river or stream and force it elsewhere, usually into a canal or **aqueduct**. Diversion dams are sometimes called weirs.

A **detention** dam is used for flood control. It is a dam that slows the speed and amount of flowing water moving downstream, sometimes holding water in a reservoir after heavy rainfall or snowmelt. It then slowly lets water move downstream after a flood threat has passed. Other dams include cofferdams—built to keep construction sites dry—and debris dams, which filter sand, gravel, or other debris from moving water.

Dams can be made from many different materials. Heavy materials, such as concrete and big rocks, stay in place because of their weight and the force of gravity.

timber

steel

rocks

In the Pipe

Storage dams create a large reservoir for future use. "Run-of-river" dams raise the water level upstream but only create a small reservoir of water there, letting the rest of the river or stream continue on.

The Modern Build

Building modern dams takes many smart engineers and scientists as well as new technology. Dam projects have four basic **phases**: investigation, design, construction, and operation and **maintenance**.

Engineers, geologists, and designers survey sites to decide whether a dam can be safely built there. Geologists study rocks and landforms, such as the canyons where dams are built. Civil engineers decide what materials can be used to create a dam. Dam designers work with these scientists to decide the type of dam needed and create blueprints for it. Engineers and architects also use math to figure out how much the dam would cost to build and maintain in the future. These studies are important because they help people decide whether a dam project would be worth the work and money.

Geologists make reports of the surrounding area. These reports are called surveys. Surveys describe the rocks and landforms that would impact the dam's construction.

Once the surveying and designing are complete and the dam is approved, work begins. In order to build a dam, the area must be dry. The river is **diverted**, usually through a tunnel or channel. Construction begins once the riverbed is dry. Extra soil and rock are removed and the dam's foundation is prepared. Holes are drilled into the ground and filled with concrete to make the foundation waterproof.

Large amounts of concrete and other materials, such as rock and clay, are brought in with dump trucks to create a solid foundation. Huge amounts of concrete are poured quickly to create the walls of most dams. Once dam construction is finished, operating the dam and maintaining it are left to specially trained scientists and structural engineers.

Engineering geologists often have to find large sources of clay, rock, and gravel nearby to help with construction.

In the Pipe

Civil engineers design many dams with roads or walkways over them. Some of these are used by workers to maintain the dams, but many are used by civilians for travel or to view the dams themselves.

Making Power

Some dams use gravity to keep water in place, and some use gravity to move water and create power. Hydroelectric power plants use water falling through tunnels to power large generators. Water is pushed by gravity through large tunnels onto a turbine. Scientists use math to determine how much water must fall from a certain height to flow through gates and move a turbine's blades, which spin and transfer power to the generator. This creates electricity.

Hydroelectric power plants create clean, reliable energy used all over the world. Because the power source—water—can be stored in a reservoir, its power generation can be saved for periods when lots of energy is needed. This period—called peak energy demand—is often in the evening.

Hydroelectric Dam

reservoir

powerhouse

power lines

generator

turbine

intake

river

Peak energy demand is usually in the evening when people are home from work and school and need more energy to cook and light homes.

In the Pipe

Engineers have even found a way to use water held in a reservoir. During the day, water flows downhill through turbines to create electricity. At night, pumps send water back uphill into a reservoir for use the next day.

Reclamation

Many dams in the western United States were built by the Bureau of **Reclamation**. The United States government created the bureau in 1902. As Americans traveled and settled west, they needed water to grow crops on farms and live in growing cities. The building of dams and other reclamation projects gave jobs to people during the **Great Depression** and saw some of the largest engineering projects in the nation's history.

Today, the Bureau of Reclamation operates dams, power plants, and canals in 17 western states. Much of the water available to people living in the western United States is available thanks to the bureau. The government agency controls more than 400 dams, including the Glen Canyon Dam in Arizona and the Hoover Dam in Nevada and Arizona.

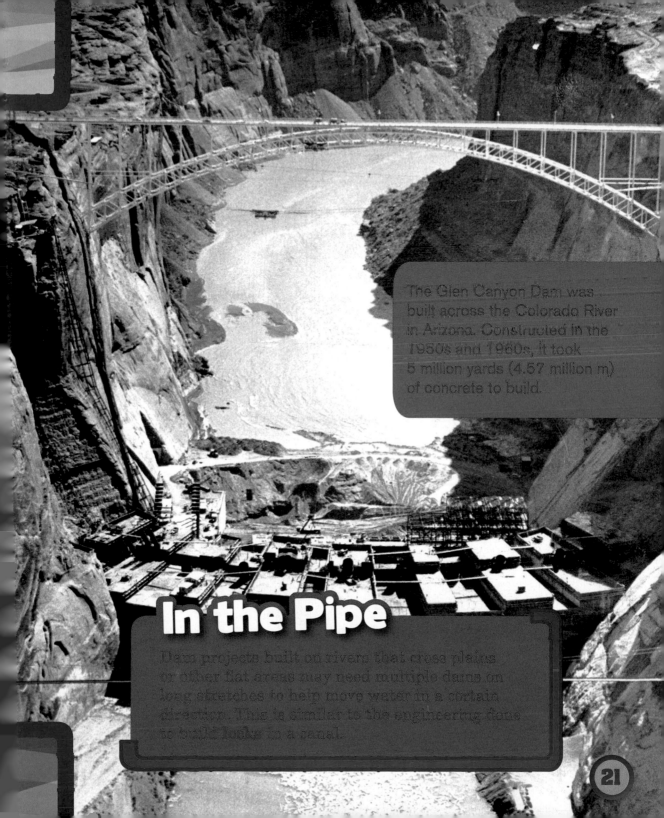

The Glen Canyon Dam was built across the Colorado River in Arizona. Constructed in the 1950s and 1960s, it took 5 million yards (4.57 million m) of concrete to build.

In the Pipe

Dam projects built on rivers that cross plains or other flat areas may need multiple dams on long stretches to help move water in a certain direction. This is similar to the engineering done to build locks in a canal.

Hoover Dam

    The most famous dam in the United States is the Hoover Dam, located on the Colorado River in Black Canyon. Inspection of the site began in the 1920s and construction began in 1931. Concrete was poured in rectangles called lifts. The lifts were cooled using cold water in pipes to speed up the hardening process. More than 5,000 people worked to build what was the largest man-made structure in the world when it was completed on September 30, 1935.

    The dam created Lake Mead, a reservoir that provides water for many states. The dam also uses water in Lake Mead to turn generators for hydroelectric power, providing electricity to cities in Arizona, California, and Nevada. The dam was officially named after President Herbert Hoover in 1947.

The Hoover Dam is as tall as a 60-story building and its base is as thick as two football fields are long!

In the Pipe

When the Hoover Dam was completed, Lake Mead was the largest man-made lake in the United States. In 2015, its reservoir sunk to a record low and many in western states worried that could impact water supplies in cities such as Las Vegas, Nevada.

Los Angeles, California, would not be the city it is today if not for William Mulholland. The self-taught engineer became head of the Department of Water and Power in Los Angeles. He created a plan to divert water from the Owens River in California to Los Angeles through a series of aqueducts and dams. The Los Angeles Aqueduct was finished in 1913 and the city soon flourished. The project was hailed as one of the greatest engineering feats of the 20th century.

In 1928, another dam Mulholland designed, the St. Francis Dam, collapsed. It released 15 billion gallons (56.8 billion l) of water. A 75-foot (22.9 m) wall of water flooded much of Ventura County and killed nearly 500 people. Mulholland resigned from his position in disgrace.

In the Pipe

Mulholland was blamed for filling the reservoir too quickly and not noticing signs that the dam was leaking. Engineers carefully study dams to make sure they are being taken care of. Otherwise they can fail.

The Lost Lake

The environmental impact of a dam can be enormous. Rerouting water with a canal or aqueduct can turn fertile farmlands into arid deserts and dry up lake beds. The Los Angeles Aqueduct and its dams have greatly harmed the Owens River valley in the decades since the aqueduct opened. With the water diverted elsewhere, the valley is plagued by dust storms and erosion.

As the population of Los Angeles swelled, more and more water was taken from the Owens River. Farmers in the area saw their crops die, and their cattle were left with nothing to graze on. Desperate to keep their farms, they even bombed the aqueduct to stop the flow of water. Even today, there are tensions surrounding water rights between Los Angeles and residents of the Owens River valley.

In the Pipe

In 2005, scientists worked to fix the problem by blocking the Los Angeles Aqueduct with a dam. This allowed the Owens River to keep flowing, controlling dust pollution from the dry lake bed and giving animals and plants a place to graze. However, the dam was removed from the lake.

Diverting water flow with dams can create large bodies of water, but it can also alter or eliminate existing waterways.

27

When Dams Fail

There are many ways a dam can fail. Bad construction and poor maintenance can cause a dam to break down. A flood can also add too much water to a reservoir, causing the dam that holds it back to weaken and break. Also, the foundation supporting a dam can move or become damaged by natural forces, such as earthquakes.

Dams that crack and break can cause massive flooding, damage to communities and animal habitats, and even deaths. Maintaining a dam is an ongoing process. New advances in STEM help engineers learn new ways to extend the life of these engineering wonders thanks to new technology. This helps them to better provide communities with power and water, while protecting the lives of those living downstream from these massive engineering projects.

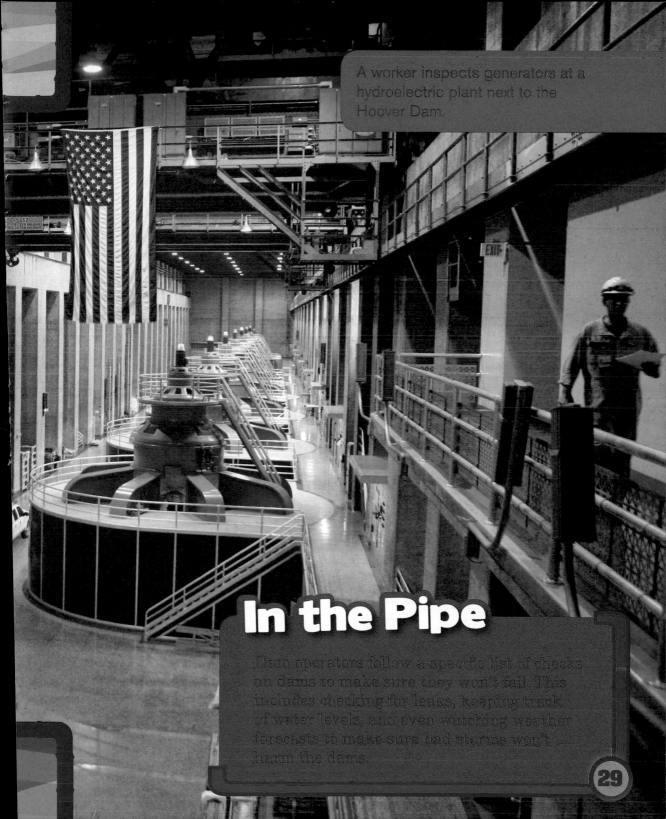

A worker inspects generators at a hydroelectric plant next to the Hoover Dam.

In the Pipe

Dam operators follow a specific list of checks on dams to make sure they won't fail. This includes checking for leaks, keeping track of water levels, and even watching weather forecasts to make sure bad storms won't harm the dams.

Changing the Landscape

Dams have a huge impact on our lives. We use the water in reservoirs for recreation, drinking, and generating power. But their construction and the reservoirs they create change the environment. Some waterways—like the Owens River—never recover from the changes dam construction brings.

As the weather and climate continue to change because of the actions of humans around the globe, scientists hope they can use dams to protect the environment from the terrible impact of global warming. Some scientists think reintroducing beavers to California could help the state recover from drought and create the wetlands needed to help improve water quality. Using the incredible power of dams may yet have a positive impact on the environment.

Glossary

aqueduct: A pathway constructed to guide water from a source into a populated area.

detention: Having to do with holding something in place.

diversion: A change in something's natural path.

divert: To change the path of something.

environment: The natural world in which a plant or animal lives.

Great Depression: A period of economic struggle in the United States and much of the world from 1929 to 1939.

hydroelectric: Relating to or used in the production of electricity by waterpower.

lock: A device for raising and lowering ships between stretches of water that are different levels.

maintenance: The act of taking care of something or maintaining it.

phase: A stage in a process or sequence of events.

reclamation: To obtain something that otherwise would be lost.

reservoir: A man-made lake used for storing water.

turbine: An engine with blades that are caused to spin by pressure from water, steam, or air.

Index

A
aqueducts, 12, 24, 26, 27

B
beavers, 4, 5, 6, 30

C
cofferdams, 12
Colorado River, 21, 22

D
debris dams, 12
Depression, Great, 20
detention dams, 12
diversion dams, 12

E
electricity, 4, 6, 18, 19, 22
engineers, 11, 14, 16, 17, 19, 24, 25, 28

G
geologists, 14, 15, 16
Glen Canyon Dam, 20, 21
gravity dams, 8, 18

H
Hoover Dam, 20, 22, 23

L
Lake Homs Dam, 8
Lake Mead, 22, 23
Las Vegas, 23
Los Angeles, 24, 26
Los Angeles Aqueduct, 24, 26, 27

M
Mulholland, William, 24, 25

O
Owens River, 24, 25, 26, 27, 30

P
peak energy demand, 18, 19
Proserpina Dam, 8

R
Reclamation, Bureau of, 20
reservoirs, 6, 7, 8, 12, 13, 18, 19, 22, 23, 25, 28, 30
Romans, 8
"run-of-river" dams, 13

S
Spain, 8
spillways, 10, 11
sluice, 10, 11
St. Francis Dam, 24, 25
storage dams, 12, 13
surveys, 15
Syria, 8

T
turbines, 6, 18, 19

W
wetlands, 6

Websites

Due to the changing nature of Internet links, PowerKids Press has developed an online list of websites related to the subject of this book. This site is updated regularly. Please use this link to access the list: www.powerkidslinks.com/sww/dams

EXPLORING COUNTRIES

Morocco

by Walter Simmons

Germantown Elementary
Media Center

BLASTOFF!
5
READERS

BELLWETHER MEDIA · MINNEAPOLIS, MN

Note to Librarians, Teachers, and Parents:

Blastoff! Readers are carefully developed by literacy experts and combine standards-based content with developmentally appropriate text.

Level 1 provides the most support through repetition of high-frequency words, light text, predictable sentence patterns, and strong visual support.

Level 2 offers early readers a bit more challenge through varied simple sentences, increased text load, and less repetition of high-frequency words.

Level 3 advances early-fluent readers toward fluency through increased text and concept load, less reliance on visuals, longer sentences, and more literary language.

Level 4 builds reading stamina by providing more text per page, increased use of punctuation, greater variation In sentence patterns, and increasingly challenging vocabulary.

Level 5 encourages children to move from "learning to read" to "reading to learn" by providing even more text, varied writing styles, and less familiar topics.

Whichever book is right for your reader, Blastoff! Readers are the perfect books to build confidence and encourage a love of reading that will last a lifetime!

This edition first published in 2012 by Bellwether Media, Inc.

No part of this publication may be reproduced in whole or in part without written permission of the publisher. For information regarding permission, write to Bellwether Media, Inc., Attention: Permissions Department, 5357 Penn Avenue South, Minneapolis, MN 55419.

Library of Congress Cataloging-in-Publication Data

Simmons, Walter (Walter G.)
 Morocco / by Walter Simmons.
   p. cm. – (Blastoff! readers: Exploring countries)
 Summary: "Developed by literacy experts for students in grades three through seven, this book introduces young readers to the geography and culture of Morocco"–Provided by publisher.
 Includes bibliographical references and index.
 ISBN 978-1-60014-731-9 (hardcover : alk. paper)
 1. Morocco–Juvenile literature. 2. Morocco–Social life and customs–Juvenile literature. I. Title.
DT305.S54 2012
964–dc23   2011032702

Printed in the United States of America, North Mankato, MN.

010112   1203

Contents

Where Is Morocco?   4
The Land   6
The Atlas Mountains   8
Wildlife   10
The People   12
Daily Life   14
Going to School   16
Working   18
Playing   20
Food   22
Holidays   24
Fez   26
Fast Facts   28
Glossary   30
To Learn More   31
Index   32

Where Is Morocco?

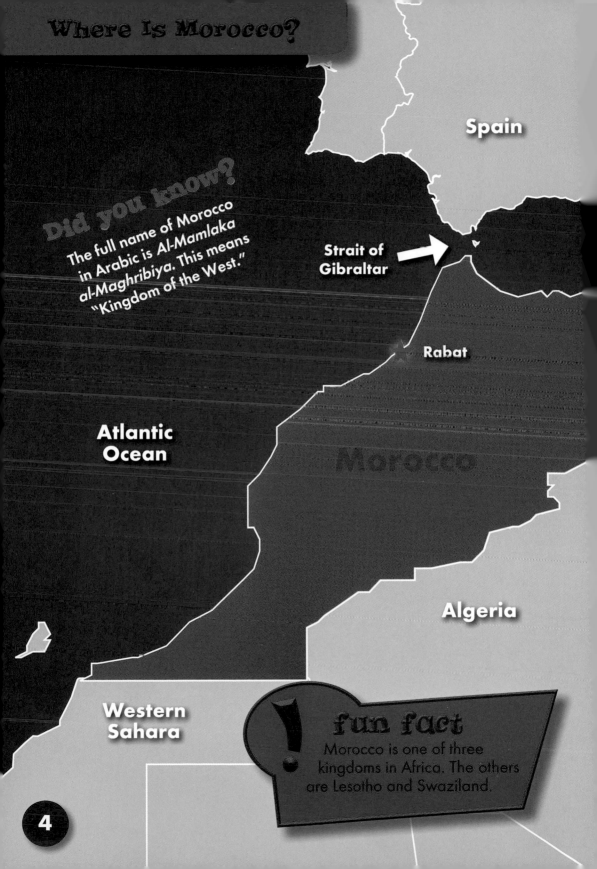

Did you know?
The full name of Morocco in Arabic is Al-Mamlaka al-Maghribiya. This means "Kingdom of the West."

Spain

Strait of Gibraltar

Rabat

Atlantic Ocean

Morocco

Algeria

Western Sahara

! fun fact
Morocco is one of three kingdoms in Africa. The others are Lesotho and Swaziland.

Mediterranean Sea

N

W ★ E

S

Morocco lies in the northwestern corner of Africa and covers 172,414 square miles (446,550 square kilometers). Algeria is Morocco's eastern neighbor. To the south is Western Sahara, which Morocco controls.

Rabat, Morocco's capital, lies on the long western coast facing the Atlantic Ocean. To the northeast is the Mediterranean Sea. The **Strait** of Gibraltar separates the Atlantic and the Mediterranean. Here the northern coast of Morocco lies just 8 miles (13 kilometers) from Spain.

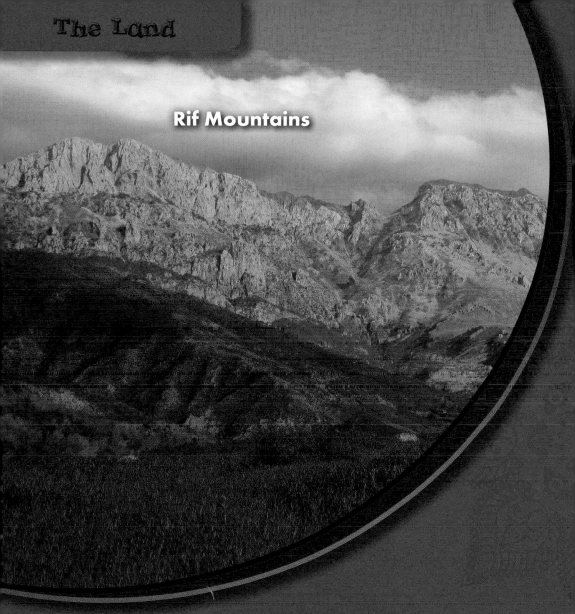

Rif Mountains

Morocco is a land of mountains, plains, and deserts.
The Atlas Mountains begin in southern Morocco.
This range stretches across the border into Algeria.
The **limestone** peaks of the Rif Mountains rise in
northern Morocco. **Fertile** lowlands separate the
Rif Mountains from the Mediterranean Sea.

The Sahara Desert covers eastern and southern Morocco. The desert continues across the northern half of Africa. Few people live or work in the Sahara, which gets very little rainfall. Summer temperatures in the desert often reach 120 degrees Fahrenheit (49 degrees Celsius).

Did you know?
Sahara means "wilderness" in Arabic.

Sahara Desert

The Atlas Mountains

Three different ranges make up
Morocco's Atlas Mountains.
The High Atlas range lies in the
center of Morocco. The Anti-Atlas
range stretches across the southern
half of the country. The Middle
Atlas is in the north.

The country's highest point,
Mount Toubkal, is in the High
Atlas and reaches a height of
13,665 feet (4,165 meters).
Forests of oak, cedar, cork,
olive, and pine trees grow on
the mountain slopes. There is
little rain, but snow falls on the
mountains in winter.

Middle Atlas Mountains

Did you know?

The Atlas Mountains formed millions of years ago, when the continents of Africa and North America collided. The Appalachian Mountains in the United States form the western half of this ancient range.

fun fact

The leaves and fruit of the argan tree attract Morocco's tree-climbing goats. These animals can easily scamper up and down tree trunks. They balance on slender branches while taking their lunch.

Dry deserts and high mountains in Morocco provide natural **habitats** for many different animals. Mouflon sheep climb high into the mountains. Antelope, deer, and gazelles prefer the plains and mountain valleys.

Barbary lions once roamed Morocco's Atlas Mountains. Though these large, powerful lions are extinct in the wild today, they still serve as a symbol of Morocco.

jerboa

cobra

houbara

In the Sahara, jackals, **jerboas**, and desert hares compete for food and water. Most **species** are active only at night when the temperature is cooler. Many reptiles, including cobras and chameleons, live in cool dens underground. Along the seacoast, marshes provide nesting ground for herons, egrets, ducks, and the houbara, a brown bird that looks like a duck with long legs.

Morocco is home to around 32 million people. The major people groups are **Arabs** and **Berbers**. Most of the people in Morocco follow **Islam** and speak the Arabic **dialect** of Darija. However, French is often used in business and the media.

Arabs and Berbers have lived in Morocco for over 1,000 years. About one out of every three Moroccans speaks a Berber language. Many Berbers live in the Atlas Mountains. Most raise crops or tend herds of sheep and goats. Some Berbers still live as **nomads**, moving from one place to another as the seasons change.

Speak Darija!

Darija is written in script. However, Darija words can be written in English to help you read them out loud.

English	Darija	How to say it
hello	ahlan	AH-lan
good-bye	bislama	bis-LA-ma
yes	eya	AY-ah
no	la	laa
please	`afek	aa-feck
thank you	shukran	SHOOK-ran
friend (male)	saheb	sah-HEEB
friend (female)	sahba	sah-BAH

medina

fun fact

A *riad* is a traditional Moroccan house. There are no windows facing the street, only a door. The family gathers in a courtyard that has a small garden or a fountain.

The **medina** is a busy place in a Moroccan city. This is the old center of town, where the streets are narrow and crowded. People walk or use motorbikes to get around. In a **souk**, stalls offer food and household goods. Umbrellas or tents shield people from the hot sun. Small workshops offer furniture, carpets, and cookware.

Stone or brick homes are common in the countryside. Older towns are surrounded by stone walls originally built to keep out desert raiders. In the desert, **oases** provide fresh water for villagers and their crops. Some Berber families live in tents made of goatskin. They pack up the tents when they move from place to place.

Where People Live in Morocco

countryside
42%

cities
58%

Did you know?

Morocco was once a colony of France. Many universities in Morocco still teach courses in French.

In Morocco, kids begin school around age 7. Primary school lasts for six years. Students study math, science, and Islam. Some also learn English or French. They then enroll at a *collège*. This is the French word for "middle school." It lasts for three years.

The next step is three years of high school. Students focus on a subject area that will prepare them for university. Some move on to one of Morocco's universities after high school. Others attend technical schools that prepare students for skilled jobs in fields such as computer programming or auto mechanics.

Where People Work in Morocco

manufacturing 20%

farming 45%

services 35%

Moroccan workers make textiles, leather goods, cement, food products, and machinery. The country is one of the world's biggest producers of phosphate. Factory workers process this natural chemical into **fertilizer**. Fishing is also important in Morocco. The catch includes sardines, tuna, anchovies, and shellfish. The country **exports** its seafood all over the world.

Farmers grow fruits, vegetables, olives, and grains. The climate is dry in Morocco, and the country often suffers **drought**. Many farms depend on canals, which bring fresh water from underground **aquifers**. The oases of the desert support the growth of dates, citrus fruits, and livestock.

19

Soccer is the favorite sport in Morocco. Kids play it on grass and dirt fields, or in the streets. Most villages and towns have a soccer field. As many as 67,000 soccer fans often pack into the Mohammed V Stadium in Casablanca. Moroccans also enjoy horse racing and playing polo. In this sport, two teams on horseback compete to drive a wooden ball into the other team's goal.

On the seacoast, people swim, surf, and sail. On the slopes of the Atlas Mountains, several resorts welcome downhill skiers. Many Moroccans also enjoy board games, including **backgammon** and chess. *Zamma* and *kharbaga* are other popular board games. Players move and capture pieces on a square board, much like checkers.

fun fact

Camel racing is popular in Morocco's Sahara region. The biggest camel race in history took place in Western Sahara. The race included 468 Arabian and Bactrian camels.

COUSCOUS

In Morocco, dinner is the big meal of the day. People sit around a low table and take food from bowls with bread or their hands. Many cooks prepare **couscous** or rice to go with meat and vegetables.

B'stilla is a pastry filled with chicken or pigeon meat, eggs, and almonds. Moroccans also enjoy *Méchoui*, which is lamb roasted on a **spit**. Another Moroccan specialty is *tagine*. This slow-cooked stew features meat, vegetables, and spices.

Moroccans love to drink hot tea flavored with mint. Coffee appears in small cups, often mixed with hot milk. Vendors on the street sell many kinds of juices and *sharbat*. They make this cool drink with milk, ice, and fruit.

tagine

hot tea

moussem of Tan Tan

Most Moroccans celebrate Islamic holidays. Muharram is the first month of the Islamic calendar. People celebrate by opening their doors and offering mint tea, almonds, and dates to visitors. Moroccans also celebrate the birth of the Prophet Muhammad, the founder of Islam. Once a year, many towns hold a local festival called a *moussem*. In the town of Tan Tan, the *moussem* features a camel market and camel races.

Independence Day takes place on November 18. Morocco won its freedom from France on this day in 1956. On July 30, Morocco celebrates Throne Day. This marks the date that King Mohammed VI took power in 1999. The king appears on television to speak to the nation. Parades also take place in cities and towns all over Morocco.

Throne Day

25

The second-largest city in Morocco is Fez. It is more than 1,200 years old and one of the country's four **imperial cities**. The others are Rabat, Marrakech, and Meknes.

A busy medina lies at the center of Fez. The Blue Gate marks its entrance, and a tall stone wall surrounds it. No cars are allowed inside. More than 9,000 narrow streets form a confusing maze within the walls. Shoppers who navigate the streets are immersed in Moroccan culture. Fez gives them an authentic taste of Morocco.

fun fact

Fez is famous for its hats. A "fez" is a tall felt hat in the shape of a cylinder. The hat is red with a tassel on top.

Blue Gate

Fast Facts About Morocco

Morocco's Flag

The flag of Morocco has a red background with a five-pointed star in the middle. The red color stands for the Alaouite Dynasty that rules Morocco. The star is a symbol of the five pillars of Islam. Morocco adopted its national flag in 1915.

Official Name: Kingdom of Morocco

Area: 172,414 square miles (446,550 square kilometers); Morocco is the 58th largest country in the world.

Capital City:	Rabat
Important Cities:	Casablanca, Agadir, Fez, Marrakech, Meknes, Tangier
Population:	31,968,361 (July 2011)
Official Language:	Arabic
National Holiday:	Throne Day (July 30)
Religions:	Muslim (98.7%), Christian (1.1%), Jewish (0.2%)
Major Industries:	farming, fishing, manufacturing, services, tourism
Natural Resources:	phosphate, fish, copper, lead, manganese, salt, iron ore, silver
Manufactured Products:	beverages, clothing, shoes, chemicals, food products, textiles
Farm Products:	olives, dates, citrus fruits, grains, potatoes, tomatoes, sugar, livestock, dairy products
Unit of Money:	Dirham; the Dirham is divided into 100 centimes.

Glossary

aquifers—underground water sources

Arabs—a people group that lives in North Africa and Western Asia

backgammon—a game of skill and chance played with a board, pieces known as checkers, and dice

Berbers—a people group originally from northwestern Africa

couscous—a grain served with many Moroccan meals

dialect—a regional variety of a language

drought—a long period of no rain

exports—sells and sends to another country

fertile—supports growth

fertilizer—a substance that helps plants grow

habitats—the environments in which a plant or animal usually lives

imperial cities—historic cities that were once home to Moroccan rulers

Islam—a religion that follows the teachings of the Prophet Muhammad

jerboas—desert rats that live in burrows and can hop long distances

limestone—a hard stone used in construction; limestone is formed over millions of years from old coral and shells.

medina—the old center of a North African city

nomads—people who have no specific home and travel from place to place

oases—fertile areas in an otherwise dry region; most oases have a spring of water.

souk—a public marketplace in Africa or the Middle East

species—specific kinds of living things; members of a species share the same characteristics.

spit—a rotating grill for cooking food

strait—a narrow stretch of water that connects two larger bodies of water

To Learn More

AT THE LIBRARY

DiPiazza, Francesca. *Morocco in Pictures.*
Minneapolis, Minn.: The Lerner Group
Twenty-First Century Books, 2007.

Merrick, Patrick. *Morocco.* Chanhassen, Minn.:
Child's World, 2000.

Seward, Pat, and Orin Hargraves. *Morocco.*
New York, N.Y.: Marshall Cavendish Benchmark,
2006.

ON THE WEB

Learning more about Morocco
is as easy as 1, 2, 3.

1. Go to www.factsurfer.com.

2. Enter "Morocco" into the search box.

3. Click the "Surf" button and you will see a list of
   related Web sites.

With factsurfer.com, finding more information is just
a click away.

Index

activities, 21
Atlas Mountains, 6, 8-9, 11, 13, 21
Blue Gate, 26, 27
capital (see Rabat)
Casablanca, 20
daily life, 14-15
education, 16-17
Fez, 26-27
food, 18, 22-23
holidays, 24-25
housing, 14, 15
imperial cities, 26
Independence Day, 25
Islam, 13, 16, 24
landscape, 6-9
languages, 4, 7, 13, 16
location, 4-5
Mount Toubkal, 8
peoples, 12-13, 15
Prophet Muhammad, 24
Rabat, 4, 5, 26
Rif Mountains, 6
Sahara Desert, 7, 11, 21
sports, 20, 21
Strait of Gibraltar, 4, 5
Tan Tan, 24

Throne Day, 25
transportation, 14
Western Sahara, 4, 5, 21
wildlife, 10-11
working, 18-19